Getting There

At American Reading Company, we believe that reading success is the cornerstone of society-wide successes, both large and small. We believe the way to open a child to the possibilities of the world is through the power of books. To that end, our goal is to enable children to read—independently—for an hour each day. We are a resource to help schools and teachers accomplish that goal swiftly and effectively.

Our most notable program, 100 Book Challenge, is our own proprietary independent reading program that has helped schools all over the country dramatically improve reading scores among their students, regardless of reading level.

Book design by Gareth Harte

First Edition, February 2006
ISBN 1-59301-264-0

AMERICAN
READING COMPANY
Independence. One book at a time.

www.americanreading.com

Getting There

By Trace Taylor
and Gina Zorzi

car

motorcycle

bus

train

6

bike

van

plane

tractor

Jeep

truck

Y: Skills Card

Reader _____ Room _____

Strategies	Date:		
"Read" by myself.			
Look at the picture for clues.			
Point at the first letter of a word.			
Get my mouth ready to make first letter sounds.			
Say a word that matches my mouth and the picture.			
Tell someone what the book was about.			
Read at home every night.			

I can get my mouth ready for

b	c	d
f	g	h
j	k	l
m	n	p
r	s	t
v	w	z

Can you match the words
to the pictures?

plane

van

truck

motorcycle

Transportation Facts

Transportation is the name for all of the ways that we can get from place to place. There are different types of transportation. Some have motors and some don't. Some have wheels and some don't. Even a person's feet are a kind of transportation.

Some kinds of transportation take effort from the people riding them. You have to pedal a bike. You have to push a skateboard. If you don't, the bike or skateboard won't get you very far.

Some kinds of transportation are pulled by animals or people, like wagons and rickshaws.

Some kinds of transportation, like cars, trains, and airplanes, use motors to move. These are called motor vehicles.

The very first plans for a motor vehicle were drawn by Leonardo da Vinci in the 1480's.

The first motor vehicle was built in 1796 by a Frenchman named Nicholas-Joseph Cugnot. It was a 3-wheeled tractor. The tractor's fastest speed was 2½ miles per hour. The tractor used steam to run its motor.